"It's okay to be broken...

Just know you can't stay there."

KATINA M. DAVIS

To request permissions, contact the author at: katina.davis88@gmail.com

ISBN: 9798795815954

Printed & Published: BWE Publishing and Consulting in the USA.

BWE Publishing and Consulting

4501 New Bern Ave STE 130-Box 144

Raleigh NC 27610

I would like to dedicate this book to my three beautiful children.

Anieya, Autumn and Kaiden: you three are my world. You are the best thing that ever happened to me and don't you ever forget it. You all make me so proud in different ways. That's what makes each of you so special. You are individuals, you are your own person and it is absolutely okay to just be who YOU are. You are enough. You will always be enough. Thank you for choosing me.

Love,

Mom

Table Of Contents

Introduction

Hey you! I know what you're thinking. "Oh great, another self-help book." I get it. Self-help books are at times boring and hard to read. Which is why YOU are in luck! This isn't just another self-help book. This is a literary piece about survival, strength, perseverance, courage, and finding confidence after experiencing domestic violence. This is a book about how I personally survived and now, I am going to share my experience to help you.

My name is Katina. I am a 33-year-old mother of three, and I SUR-VIVED. I do not like to use the word "story" when referring to what I've been through. Let me explain why. By definition, a story is "an account of imaginary or real people told for entertainment." Nothing about what I've been through is entertaining. Nothing about what any survivor has been through is entertaining. We have been through a hellish ordeal; one which was daunting, demeaning, gruesome, and outright unbearable. So instead, I choose to use the words "my truth," because that's what it is. This is MY truth and no one will silence me from speaking MY TRUTH.

I met my abuser at a time when I was at the lowest point in my life. I was depressed; beyond depressed. I had just had a baby six months prior by a man that I had known since high school. He wanted absolutely nothing to do with my child. I already had two children whom I was the sole provider for, and here I am, embarking on a journey with a third child that I would

"It's okay to be broken... Just know you can't stay there."

be raising all alone. I want to make it abundantly clear that I love my baby. I love all my babies and I am so proud of the bright-eyed child that God destined to be mine from that situation. I had to add that in case he ever reads this book.

Anyway, when I met my abuser, it was like he could smell the weakness on me. Did you read that? Read it again, because it is very much relevant to many components of this book. HE COULD SMELL THE WEAKNESS ON ME. I lacked self-worth, self-love, and self-awareness. Oh, at that time, I just lacked innumerable characteristics that a thirty-year-old woman that is sure of herself should possess. He worked in the same building that I worked in but for a different company. It was a café and it was directly next to my job. Being that I was a single parent, I would pick my two daughters up from school on my lunch break at three pm every day and let them sit in the café next door to finish up homework while I finished the remainder of my day. Each time I would go to the café, I would notice him just staring at me with this half-cocked smile. I'll admit I thought he was handsome but, I honestly refused to give the man the time of day due to where I was in my own life. I just did not want to be bothered. I knew that I wasn't at the best version of myself, and I just wanted to stay by myself at that point. When I was inside the café, he would press his head up against the glass window with his hands cupped around his face to block out the sun, just to stare at me. Eventually, he asked me if he could buy my kids some snacks. God, why did I say yes? This was the only window he needed to creep in and spin his web. His contrivance to have me was like something I had never seen.

From that day forward, his advances became more intense and more frequent. I continued to shoot him down, in-spite of his efforts. He even waltzed right into my job one day and brought me lunch and a bouquet of flowers. I turned him down again, even on that day. Now, let me pause for a minute, because I want you to understand that this persistence was both love bombing and a red flag. Love bombing is "an attempt to influence a person by demonstrations of attention and affection." The pursuer will go out of their way to overwhelm the victim with loving words or loving actions coupled with manipulative behaviors. At this point, I had already told him no several times, but he persisted. The persistence should have been the red flag, and when you learn how my truth ends in this situation, you will begin to connect the dots like I did. He showed me who he was from the very beginning, I just didn't pick up on the signs. I must admit that the negative space that I was in was not the only reason that I turned him down. He met me at a time where I was transitioning and relocating to another state. "I'm about to move. It won't work with him anyway," I thought. Until one day, I guess he just caught me on the right day. I finally gave in to his advances and agreed to go on a date with him. "I will probably never see this man again. Why not go have some fun before I leave town? Oh, the hell with it. Yes, I will go on a date with you." Unbeknownst to me, this was the beginning of the worst experience of my life. The pathway to a living hell. I hope that my writing this book will encourage another survivor out there to choose herself, love herself, breathe life back into herself and embark on the rewarding yet challenging journey of healing and self discovery. It's a beautiful journey. Pay close attention and write a few things down if you must. I don't want you to miss anything.

Chapter 1: Confidence: How I lost it and how I gained it back

Our first date was nothing short of amazing. He was funny, charismatic, caring, genuine, hardworking, thoughtful, and street smart. All the components of a perfect man, or so I thought. Our first date occurred at an "Escape Room." We laughed, we smoked our herbs, we sipped our drinks, and we just were having an amazing time. When we left, it was pouring rain. I had to park about three blocks away because there was no parking, only on-street parking. This man walked all the way to my car in the pouring rain just to grab my umbrella from the trunk. He was soaking wet, but he returned with the umbrella post-haste so that I wouldn't get wet. We went on a few more dates prior to my leaving the state and by that time, I hadn't noticed any red flags or anything else that would alert me to the type of person he really was. He was just perfect. That was the last time I ever saw that funny, charismatic, caring, genuine, hardworking, thoughtful man. After that, all hell broke loose.

After my transition out of state, we continued to date long distance. He would come and visit until eventually, he transitioned out of state altogether to be with me. Now, he was very familiar with the new state that I had moved to, as he had resided there for a short period of time with his mother in the 90s. I revealed that I was moving very early on in the relationship, and I do believe he used that to further connect with me because he had lived

"It's okay to be broken… Just know you can't stay there."

there before. He preyed on me from the very beginning. When he would come to visit me before he made his move out of state, he would make it seem that he was in town to visit old acquaintances and family members, which I later learned were lies. His family and friends wanted nothing to do with him due to his erratic behavior, which I would also soon learn the hard way. The abuse didn't begin as physical abuse; that part didn't start until I came to my senses and realized what I had gotten myself into. What I experienced toward the beginning of the relationship was Emotional Abuse. *Allow me to pause here for a moment, because just as I didn't realize I was being emotionally abused, I'm sure one of my readers may have overlooked it just like I did. Please understand that a person does not have to be putting their hands on you to be abusing you. Emotional abuse is "a form of controlling another person by using emotions to criticize, embarrass, shame, blame or otherwise manipulate that person." Do you recognize these behaviors in your partner? If so, leave now. I am a living testament that things will not get any better. I have never been in an abusive relationship prior to this situation so, it was not easy for me to recognize that what was happening to me was in fact abuse.* Things were not going as planned with my relocation as far as my job- our stability was shaky, and my son became ill. About three months into my relocation, things just began to fall apart. However, he stayed by my side through it all and made sure that I never forgot that he did. He would say things to me daily like, "You're lucky I'm even with you. You have three kids and their fathers don't even help you. Ain't nobody going to put up with this." Remember how I told you that when I met him, I was depressed and at the very worst version of myself? Well, someone in that state of mind would be very easy to manipulate and quite frankly, they would also easily wager their own self-worth and happiness for someone else. Which is why it is important to stay by yourself until you are healthy and whole. Daily, he would tear me down and destroy my confidence even more. Some days, I felt like I wasn't even worthy of walking the earth. That's how low he made me feel.

I remember the very first day that I saw his anger emerge. We were between homes and were in the middle of moving. Everything was a mess; clothes were mixed up and in the wrong place and everything was all out of sorts. We went to McDonald's to grab breakfast, and that is when he noticed that my oldest daughter had on a pair of his pants. She had mistaken them for her pants due to everything being in such disarray. It pains me to even recollect his reaction and behavior that day. I can't bring myself to repeat it in this book because as a mother, it hurts me to the core. The things he said to her were outright unacceptable, and please believe I didn't stand for it. In fact, everyone in the McDonald's was behind me and in full attack mode. Two men had stepped in front of me and were ready to mop the floor with him. That is the very first day I realized who he truly was and what I had gotten myself into. No one in their right mind would speak to a child like that. All this, over some pants? I had to put my daughter in therapy behind that incident alone. It's one thing to abuse me, but what you won't do is do this to my child.

I still blame myself for that day. No matter what anyone says, I brought this man into our lives and he nearly emotionally destroyed us all. Some may ask, well, why didn't you leave that day? Anyone who has been in an abusive relationship can tell you that this question is one, inappropriate, and two, insensitive. Abusive relationships are about power and control. If it were that easy for us to leave, don't you think that we would? What we go through with our abusers is called a "Cycle of Abuse." *The Cycle of Abuse typically has four stages: Building Tension, An Incident of Abuse, Reconciliation, and Calm.* He would blame his mounting tension on the fact that so many things did not go according to plan and as a man, he felt that he was lacking in providing for his "family." I soon learned that his behavior stemmed from his own unhappiness about his shortcomings and where he was in his life as a thirty-nine-year-old man, as well as a diagnosed mental illness for which he was supposed to be taking prescribed medication.

Soon after he would express to me his frustrations, he'd start an argument, verbally abuse me, and then gaslight me to make it seem like I was the cause of the argument and everything was my fault. *Do you know what gaslighting is? That's when someone manipulates another person into questioning their own sanity. Imagine going through that every single day for two whole years. It was so bad that I would really sit and try to figure out what I had done to cause this and eventually, I realized he was creating a false reality.* I felt like I was losing my damn mind. After he would abuse me emotionally, he would do something to reconcile such as being overly gentle and kind with his words, gifting me with something, or even displaying physical affection. Mind you, he only displayed physical affection when HE felt like it or when it was convenient for him. Anytime I would try to touch him, he would say, "Come on, boo. Get off me, I ain't in the mood." Just completely and utterly insensitive. However, after he abused me, then he would suddenly get in touch with his soft side. He would apologize but never really take full accountability. It would always be something that I did to "make him act that way," and things would be calm for maybe a full day, and then the abuse started again. What I just described to you is the cycle of abuse and how easy it is to fall into.

This went on for some time. Every day was uncomfortable, unbearable. I remember watching my kids' facial expressions change after they got off the school bus. I would watch as they both laughed and said goodbye to their friends and, the minute they turned toward home there was a look of sorrow and disinclination. I saw just how completely regretful they were that they had to come home. It made my stomach turn. Can you imagine? Your children not even wanting to come home? A place that is supposed to be happy and safe. By this time, things were extremely bad. Our home was not a happy one. We argued every single day. He had completely stripped me of my CONFIDENCE, and my self-esteem, everything that a woman is supposed to feel about herself, I lacked. That is until things started to come together for me.

I was having a hard time finding employment. The job market was difficult at the time because the city was and still is severely overpopulated and for every one position, there were over 30 applicants waiting to interview after you. I remember going to an interview and seeing more than 20 people in the lobby. It was crazy. Of course, I didn't go to the interview by myself. He was in the car waiting. *An abuser very rarely allows you to have time outside of them because they are afraid that you will leave or be influenced by others to leave.* He had his hooks into me. I did get the job that day but had to turn it down because it did not offer benefits. That was when I decided to post in a Mom's group on Facebook and ask if anyone had any connections on employment. My current boss stepped into the comments and told me to inbox her. At the time, I didn't know what the conversation would be but, before I could inbox her, she had inboxed me. Her talk was that of a God-fearing woman; one of faith and strong prayer. She said, and I will never forget it, "I don't know you or your story, but something tells me to take a chance on you. I am willing to extend this olive branch to you and get you the interview, but the rest is on you." I interviewed and shortly after, I was hired. I remain employed there to this day and I thank God for her being the ram in the bush. I was doing some heavy praying during this time in my life. I mean, praying like nobody's business, and I am certain that no one other than God led me to her. Without her giving me that chance, I may not have regained my confidence and found the strength, resources, and courage to leave. Had I not found that job, I may honestly be dead. Either he would have killed me or I'd have killed myself.

It was in the same Mom's group that I also met a close friend of mine who became an integral part of my survival journey, my life, and my truth. We will just call her Jaz. It's funny how God works. When I met up with Jaz for the first time, she asked where I lived. When I told her, she said, "You live in unit 17? That townhouse where the dude is always sitting on the porch singing?" *You see, my abuser was a singer. That was part of the way he wooed me. He could sing the panties off me if I'm just being honest. He was unemployed at the time and would sit on the front porch, listen to Pandora and sing, all day. It was so embarrassing because I was going to work every single day, while this man was sitting on the porch singing.* Anyway, I said, "Yes, I live in 17." She replied, "My mom lives right across from you. She's the one whose town house was broken into last week." This was nothing but God because Jaz and her mother sheltered myself and my kids many times in the coming months when my own home was unsafe. I was in a new state where I knew no one and just like that, God not only placed help in my path but right at my front door. Jaz wasn't just someone who I called to seek shelter. She was genuinely my friend. We clicked immediately and she helped to breathe life back into me. She was pouring into me daily. Reminding me of my worth, encouraging me that I am better than this situation, that I am beautiful, smart, and kind. With her help and the help of my affirmations, I was starting to feel like myself again.

Chapter 1: Confidence: How I lost it and how I gained it back

Every morning before work I would get up, get in the mirror, and say my daily affirmations. "I am smart. I am courageous. I am beautiful. I am capable. I am loved. I am worthy of love. I am worthy of love that doesn't hurt." For those of you that may not be familiar with affirmations, affirmations are the acts or processes of affirming something or being affirmed. Other definitions may define affirmations as emotional support or encouragement. It may seem as though something so simple and minute could not possibly make a difference to such a damaged psyche but, I assure you that it will. The more you look at yourself in the mirror and say these statements to yourself, the more they begin to resonate with you, and the more you begin to believe and embody the things you are speaking. You must speak life into yourself. If you are in an abusive relationship, please make daily affirmations a part of your journey to rebuilding your confidence, self-love, and self-awareness. I had also started to wear makeup again, something that I genuinely enjoyed but was talked out of by my abuser. He would say things like, "Oh, you don't need that. You are beautiful the way you are." He didn't want me wearing clothes that were too revealing or showing of my shape because of his own insecurities and need to control me. It was not because he believed I was beautiful at all. Sound familiar? I remember one day he literally ripped a dress off of me because I refused to change my clothes. He said it was "too sexy." I expressed that I knew it was sexy and that I wanted to feel pretty and attractive on that particular day. He grabbed me by my neck and held me up against the wall while he used his other hand to begin ripping at the dress and tearing it off me. I cried something serious that morning. I mean I cried the entire way to work. I didn't let that incident stop me or change who I was becoming though. I was determined to be me again. I didn't want to live life as this version of Katina.

"It's okay to be broken… Just know you can't stay there."

Once I started to affirm myself, put my makeup on, and dress the way I liked to dress again, he became angry. He didn't like that. I was flourishing and coming out of my dark place, but he was staying stagnant and quite frankly, it pissed him off. *What gave me the right to better myself and leave him where he was? Who did I think I was?* This was when the physical abuse started and when I found the strength and confidence to start fighting back instead of being his emotional and physical punching bag. This was when I knew it was time to develop a safety plan and get out.

This next chapter may be a trigger warning. Brace yourself as I outline the chain of events that led me to develop a safety plan and the journey to making it out. It was not easy. In fact, it was the most tumultuous thing that ever occurred in my life, but I did it. You can too. Everyone's journey is different and you may find that your road is easier or more difficult than mine. However, the components of what it takes to make it out of an abusive relationship are all the same. Leaving an abusive relationship requires strength, courage, bravery, and, most of all, CONFIDENCE in yourself. Confidence is "a feeling of self-assurance arising from one's appreciation of your own abilities or qualities." This is why it is important to do everything you can to build yourself back up mentally throughout the abusive relationship no matter how difficult it may be, so that you can believe in yourself enough to safely remove yourself from that terrible situation.

I AM BEAUTIFUL

Use the spaces below to uplift yourself. Write down a list of charac-

teristics that you love about YOU. Write until you run out of space.

_____

_____

_____

_____

_____

_____

_____

_____

_____

_____

_____

_____

_____

_____

_____

_____

_____

_____

_____

_____

_____

_____

_____

Chapter 2: Safety Planning

Safety Planning is crucial when you are attempting to make an escape from an abusive relationship. *Safety Planning is the act of forming a plan to exit the relationship, which significantly reduces the risk of harm to the victim. A survivor is most in danger when he/she is attempting to flee the relationship and during the first three months after exiting the relationship.* My abuser was clingy. I mean, he just would not let go. Every step I made, he made. So, it was extremely difficult for me to develop a plan because I never had time away from him. As I stated in the last chapter, by the time I was ready to develop a safety plan, he had started putting his hands on me. His abuse had become more intense. I remember the very first time he hit me was when we were driving to Kroger to grocery shop and he had created an argument. There had been so many disagreements that I don't even remember what this particular argument was about. I had begun giving him the silent treatment and letting him argue by himself, assuming that this would diffuse the argument rapidly as opposed to arguing with him and adding fuel to his fire. Well, little did I know that when you are dealing with a narcissist, whether you argue with them or not the disagreement and extreme uncomfortability of the situation will still remain a result. So, as I was making a right turn into the Kroger parking lot, the next thing I knew, the right side of my face was stinging and the left side of my face was hitting the window. Blood leaked from my mouth like a faucet. My right ear was ringing and at the time, I was still in the middle of driving, so I had put the car in park to catch my bearings and keep from driving onto the median. We were smack dab in the middle of the entryway to the grocery store and cars had begun to pile up behind us. I got out of the car and waved my hands for others to call the police, and he got out in an attempt to drag me back into the car. At this point, it was on! I fought back. We were literally boxing in the Kroger parking lot. I ended up walking away and leaving my car right in the middle of the street along with him because at this point, he had taken the keys. He was famous for that. My goal was to get away from him and the situation as quickly as possible because I knew that once police arrived, all he would do is lie to make it seem as if he was the victim, and all the authorities would do is brush this off as another domestic dispute just as they'd done in the past.

Onlookers just watched in horror from their vehicles. I could tell they wanted to assist but were afraid for their own safety, so they remained in their cars and watched instead. There was one woman who saw me walking down the road, bloody from the encounter, and she pulled over, cleaned me up, and gave me a ride home where my kids were waiting. She made sure to stop and purchase a new shirt for me because she said, "If your children are at home, we do not want them to see you in this condition." I wish I could find that woman to properly thank her and do something nice for her. I was just too distraught to think that far ahead at that time. By this time, I had called the police so as to have a record of what had occurred. *This is very important. Always make a paper trail. This will work to your advantage if you ever need to obtain a TPO (Temporary Protective Order) or Restraining Order.* County police did respond that day and, when they did, they gave me the same spiel: "Well ma'am, we can't put him out. Legally, you can't either. If he has been a resident here more than 30 days, then he has rights even if he is not on your lease. You must file an eviction." I know what you're thinking!

The same thing I was thinking. "An eviction?! Sir, I am going through it with this man and enduring various forms of abuse from sunup to sundown, and you think I have time to wait for an eviction?" I asked. This is outrageous, I thought to myself. By this time, he still hadn't made it home but I knew that when he did, the fight would continue. So, what did I do? I checked myself and my kids into a hotel. Jaz had always opened her home to us but naturally, I did not always want to disrupt her life with my issues. So, at times, I opted to go to a hotel for a night or two instead of calling her.

A part of safety planning is saving money. Everything we do requires money, right? I had a little money set aside for days just like this when I needed an escape and had nowhere to go. Please be sure to always have enough in your account to pay for at least two nights in a hotel. This should be just enough time to find temporary housing resources and file a TPO. At this time, I knew nothing about a TPO because as I said, I'd never been in this situation before and had no idea what to do or the steps to take to protect myself. The officers never mentioned a TPO, all they mentioned was an eviction. I thought that was my only option. *In case you are feeling trapped and also don't know your options, I want to make sure that you understand that a TPO is an option for you whether the abuser lives in your home or not. TPO laws/requirements may differ by state. However, a TPO is always an option if you feel that your life is in danger.* I think I can feel your next question coming. Did I apply for the eviction? The answer is no, not immediately. Let me explain why. At the time, like many other victims, financial/economic abuse played a factor in our relationship. Due to his poor temperament and inability to control his emotions, he was unable to keep a steady job. This meant that I was the sole provider for us all. I was almost always strapped for cash. Filing an eviction isn't free. It was either I use the little money I had saved to file the eviction and stay in the home to endure abuse or, I stay at the hotel and try to find a way to file the eviction later. Like many of you, I had to put the well being of my children before my own. Many nights when arguments would ensue, it was a school night and they needed a full night's, undisturbed rest. I chose the hotel. I, too, needed to rest as I cannot function with lack of sleep.

Over the course of the next few months, the abuse became more frequent, the psychotic episodes on his behalf also increased, and my resentment and desire to get away from him continued to grow. There were days that he made me feel absolutely crazy. He would make a decision to do something and then when it did not go the way he intended, he'd turn it on me and shout at me. He would yell things like, "See, I told you I didn't want to do this!" And, I'd be sitting there looking at him like "WHAT?" I didn't have anything to do with this. I never encouraged him to do anything nor did I ever say anything about any of his decision making. I remember one day he and I decided to take a ride to Douglasville. Anytime we went somewhere, I would always drive because he did not have a license and quite frankly, I didn't trust him enough to not get erratic and drive us both into a ditch. However, on this particular morning, he insisted on driving. I allowed it because I just did not want to fight. I'd always attempt to avoid conflict at all costs. When we finally made it to our destination, the man did the unthinkable. He hit a parked car as he was trying to pull into the parking space! Yes, a parked car. The owners of the vehicle were coming out of the store and as you can imagine, they were furious. He then turned his anger on me and said, "I told you I didn't want to drive! This is your fucking fault!" All the while, I am sitting in the passenger's seat angry that this is even happening and confused as to how I became to blame for a decision that HE made. He would gaslight me all the time. This would happen every single day. It was to the point that my kids were taking on the role of comforting me and telling me, "Hey, Mom, you didn't do anything wrong. He is crazy." The minute they began taking on the role of MY caretaker is the minute I decided that I was not going to tolerate this any longer. I had to develop a plan, no matter what that plan may look like or what was at risk. It is not the job of my children to comfort me nor to take on my problems as their own. They are children; I am the adult and I'll be damned if I allow this situation to take away any more of their childhood.

I had a hotel on standby where the night clerk and I were on a first-name basis. I had her phone number. I would text her and type "911," and she would reserve my room and have it paid with my card on file by the time I got there. Why the night clerk? I was at work during the day so, most of the time, our arguments occurred in the evenings or at night. I made sure that he did not know about the hotel. He was not the type of abusive partner to go through my phone, but I know some of you don't have these same liberties. *That portion of safety planning will have to be different for you. You may need to develop a relationship with a neighbor when you take out the trash, or check the mail. You may even need to find a way to safely reach out to a close friend or family member to assist you with safety planning as their help may be needed to facilitate your escape. Safety planning is all about strategic thinking and finding holes in your abuser's schedule and plans. Those holes are your windows of opportunity.*

The plan was to move out of my apartment all together and have him come home one day, and the house be empty. I had already spoken to my leasing office about moving me to another unit on the complete opposite end of the complex. They were well aware of the situation as the constant police presence was beginning to be a nuisance. Not to mention that I lived right in front of the leasing office, which worked both to my advantage and my disadvantage. If I didn't get away from this man, I ran the risk of being evicted, thus leaving myself and my children homeless. That wasn't an option. There were two ways to get through the neighborhood and if I did this correctly, he wouldn't even know that I still resided in the complex. This was my only window of opportunity as he had taken another odd job that put him out of the house during the day. I was getting close, and he knew it too. The way I was acting toward him, my silence, my smiles in response to his anger, the way my children and I left with no warning to spend the weekend at Jaz's, and the way I fought back when he hit me, he knew that the end was near. There was no more just taking the beating for the sake of minimizing the violence in my home. I was completely and utterly tired. I had my plan in place and was set to vacate the apartment within the next month. He knew that something was going on. He just couldn't figure out what. Anytime I would leave the house, he was on his knees,crying, begging me to stay. The man was insane.

After weeks of having the police consistently show up at my apartment for disturbances, calling locksmiths to change the locks on my car because he had taken my keys to keep me from escaping, and countless nights of physical fighting, I was exhausted. Both mentally and physically. Being home had become unbearable. The abuse was escalating. *Let's pause again. It is imperative to recognize the signs of Escalation in Domestic Violence because this means the victim is more in danger than ever before. Escalation is when abuse gets worse either suddenly or gradually, and it can consist of a transition from one type of abuse to another. The abuse will typically escalate when the abuser begins to feel that he/she is losing power over the relationship. Remember, abusive relationships are all about power and control. They may feel threatened by their partner's newfound sense of independence and self-awareness and will use escalating violent behaviors as a warning sign of what could happen to their partner should they exit the relationship. This warning is not to be taken lightly as seventy-five percent of serious injuries occur once the survivor has decided to exit the abusive relationship. Hence, the importance of having a solid safety plan in place to exit the relationship safely and reduce the risk of harm to yourself and others. It may not be a good idea to take shelter at the home of someone you know or a family member because your abuser can easily find you. Do include those you trust in helping you develop a safety plan but don't make taking shelter at their home a part of that plan. In the end, it could lead to the harm or fatality of yourself as well as your loved one.*

The world had just begun to give way to the COVID-19 pandemic and stay-at-home orders had gone into effect. I was working from home. My kids were learning virtually and we were all home 24 agonizing hours per day. Every day had morphed into hell on earth. The police had been to my home multiple times per week since the implementation of the stay-at-home orders, and they continued to show the same level of injustice by not offering me resources and telling me to file an eviction to remove him. You guys know just as well as I do that evictions were grounded during the pandemic. So, where did that leave me? What could I do? I was trapped. I had everything in place to move out of my apartment and then one night, he did something drastic. I was asleep on the sofa and I woke up to my iPhone dinging. There were three text messages from him. "Why is he texting me from the room?" I asked myself. I then opened those text messages to read some of the most horrifying words I've ever read. "I'm tired of being surrounded by no love. I'm going to take this whole bottle of pills in front of everyone so everyone in this house can feel my pain. I'm going to take you with me." Take me with him, I thought to myself. Oh my God!!! This man has lost it, I thought again.

"It's okay to be broken... Just know you can't stay there."

This part right here is called LETHAL ESCALATION. I thought I was going to die that night and had all intentions of grabbing my children and going to a shelter right then and there, in the middle of the night. I put nothing past him at this point. As soon as I finished reading the text, I saw him stumbling down the hallway toward my dining room in the dark; he was making his way to the kitchen. I just watched in confusion and horror. I didn't know what to think. Suddenly, I heard one of my glasses break in the kitchen. I ran in there to see what happened and I knew immediately when I looked at him that he had really done it. He had taken an excessive amount of pills and his ability to stay conscious was fading. He screamed, "Look what you made me do!" His speech was slurred, his eyes glassy, and his mouth twisted. I was terrified. I was unable to assimilate what was happening but in that moment, my instincts kicked in and I called 911.

By the time the paramedics had arrived, I had already escorted him back to our bedroom to lie down so as to keep him from passing out and hitting his head. I pleaded with the EMT's to do whatever they needed to do quietly as my children were asleep. As they were in my bedroom attempting to perform standard procedures to save him from the inevitable, he was my least concern. I walked to each of my children's rooms and cracked the door to ensure they were still sleeping among all the commotion. To my surprise, they were all sleeping soundly. I stood in the hallway as the paramedics pleaded with him to allow them to do their jobs. I heard him screaming, "I'm not going nowhere! Leave me the fuck alone! Bring that bitch in here. She's the reason for all this. This is all her fault!" Now, had this been a year and a half ago when I was weak and easily controlled by his emotional abuse and manipulation, those words would have affected me differently. I would have believed him. Instead, I stood my ground and began to tell the paramedics that he was mentally unstable, I was being abused, and that they needed to remove him from my home. I also showed them the text messages he had sent thirty minutes prior. It was evident that he had become a danger to himself as well as everyone around him; me and my children. With that, the paramedics did their jobs and transported him to the hospital. I wasn't the slightest bit worried about him. I wasn't sad. I didn't have sympathy. The only emotion that seemed to fill me was that of relief. I was relieved that this man was gone and would finally be out of my hair. *He's his family's problem now*, I thought. I couldn't have been more wrong.

Like anyone, I assumed that he would be committed to a mental health facility, never to be released again unless he was medically evaluated and proved to be of no danger to himself or others. I assumed that I would have some time to disappear and break free. I had finally been able to get through to his family and show them the severity of all that was going on. His mother agreed to come and get him and I couldn't be more relieved. He was admitted to the hospital and his mother traveled over ten hours from out of state to visit him only for him to have an erratic episode and advise hospital personnel that he did not want to see her. She was extremely hurt behind his actions due to the distance and great lengths she'd gone to travel to see him. His behavior toward her even aggravated me because the one time that she decided to get involved, she simply couldn't. Her hands were tied. He was an adult and no one could make him do anything outside of his will. *When I had contacted her in the past, she would say she did not want to get involved due to his erratic behavior as she was up in age and battling her own illness. She couldn't take all the drama and I understood that- to a certain extent. His family had given me a "he is your problem now" vibe throughout the entire relationship, although I expressed that I desperately wanted to get away from him. The fact that his entire family and all of his acquaintances knew of his mental illness and erratic behavior but never disclosed this information to me as his girlfriend was unnerving and it really made me angry.*

Ultimately, he began to contact me from the facility, threatening that if I didn't pick him up or let him back into my home, that he would appear at my apartment complex and make a scene. The staff at the facility was also contacting me in lieu, and I made it abundantly clear to them that he was not to be released back into my care nor was he able to return to my home. The staff at that facility specifically stated that they were unable to release him unless he was released into the care of another adult. Eventually, I blocked the calls from the facility. Until one day, he contacted me and advised that he had just gotten off the bus and was waiting for me to pick him up at a local mall. He threatened that he would find a way to my house and make a scene on the property if I didn't come and pick him up. Here I was, stuck between a rock and a hard place. "What do I do?" I asked myself. Should I call the police? Of course not, all they are going to do is give me the same excuse as to why they can't remove him from the property. *If I don't go get him and he shows up here, someone will call the police*, I thought. I can't have another incident or the leasing office will file an eviction and we will have nowhere to go. I felt trapped. I felt like I didn't have any options. None of my family lived here so, who could I really call? What would you have done? For the sake of maintaining a roof over my kids' heads and wanting to avoid another incident, I reluctantly went and picked him up from the mall. When I pulled up, I remember seeing this smile on his face. It was one of cockiness and victory, as if he wanted to say "Yeah, I knew you would come. What else are you going to do?" I immediately broke down and started crying. I cried the entire way home, talking to myself and to God. "God, if you just get me out of this. Please get me out of this" I felt forsaken. I felt so alone and helpless. I had spent all this time Safety Planning and it seemed like my plan was going down the drain. He wouldn't loosen his hold on me. He just would not go away. "I'm never going to get away from this man. If I do, it will be in a box."

I AM WORTHY OF LOVE THAT DOESN'T HURT

Complete the word search below. This short puzzle contains a few words that are characteristics of a healthy relationship.

-Talk

-Respect

-Compromise

-Honesty

-Kindness

-Love

```
R  K  L  T  H  K  L  A  T  I  O  P  L
E  G  C  O  M  P  R  O  M  I  S  E  S
S  V  Y  O  U  E  J  T  L  P  V  Y  C
P  B  T  T  S  S  E  N  D  N  I  K  O
E  Z  U  P  S  H  E  T  F  R  L  Y  P
C  K  E  D  K  E  V  D  G  D  X  V  O
T  C  I  B  C  V  N  N  V  E  K  D  Q
T  H  E  Y  Y  O  I  O  Z  I  Y  W  R
U  M  R  Z  H  L  T  Y  H  U  R  F  T
```

Chapter 3: Fight For Your Life

"You've gotta be careful who you let up in your house, around your children. Sometimes people come with demons and spirits you know nothing about. It will be easy to let them in but even harder to get them out." These were the words of my Pastor/Mother at a local church that had taken us in while we were homeless. The church members showed us so much love during that dark time in my life and had it not been for that church and its head Pastor, my family probably would not be where we are today. I had called her to have a conversation one afternoon on my lunch break and I was sitting in the Kroger parking lot when she said those words to me. Those words ended our call and once I hung up, I felt chills going up my spine and the hairs raising on my arms and neck. I KNEW exactly what she was talking about and what those words meant. At that moment, I began to cry out to God. I cried out to him and said, "God, please save me. Please help me. If you get me out of this, I promise I will dedicate my life to you and make my best efforts to live my life right. I need you to get me out of this, Lord. Get me and my kids away from this man, please!" I sobbed uncontrollably in my car; not caring who was around or who saw me. I was totally surrendering myself and my problems to God because I realized that He was the only person that could fight this battle. Nothing I had done up until this point had been successful. Philippians 4:6-7 says "do not be anxious about anything, but in everything by prayer and supplication with thanksgiving let your requests be made known to God. And the peace of God, which surpasses all understanding, will guard your hearts and your minds in Christ Jesus." I was raised on God's word. I stand on God's word. I believe in God's word and on that day, I believed that he would hear my prayers and answer them. He had to. I was fading away. The very next day, it all hit the fan.

"I can't stand being in here. Tired of being stuck around you, them kids, all of it. I'm a good dude. I don't cheat on you, or none of that. Any woman out here would be happy to have a good nigga like me," he said. I was still working from home as we were about three months into the COVID-19 pandemic, and had just woken up to his complaining and angry face. He was glaring at me from the master bathroom; the vein that pops out of his forehead when he gets upset was very much visible that morning. I knew then that we were going to have a problem. "What could he possibly be angry about this early in the morning?" I asked myself. Usually, I would stay quiet, but on this particular day, I gave him a reply. Tired wasn't the word to describe how I felt that morning. I was both exasperated and repulsed by him and his behavior. Enough was enough. It was about 8:30 am and I was due to log in for work within the next thirty minutes. Then, I replied, "Leave then. Leave us right where you found us. I have been begging you to leave for months but you refuse. You walk around here and deflect your demons and shortcomings on all of us when the real problem lies within you. You're a good dude but you're whipping my ass every chance you get, tearing me down with your words, making me feel like I'm nothing, verbally abusing me in front of my children—and this is what you call being a good man?! Just get the fuck out! I assure you that we will be fine." The next thing I knew, we were going at it, nearly trying to kill one another. We had fought many times before but this fight, this one was divergent.

I was giving it everything I had to fight back and to be honest, I believe my mindset that day was "It's going to be him or me." I was fed up; with everything. I was having flashes in my mind of all the times that he'd hit me, verbally abused me, mishandled me, made my children uncomfortable in their own home; everything. Everything I had been through with him was flashing through my mind all at once in that moment. He punched me in my face and knocked me backward into the wall with such force that I hit the rear of my head against the wall. He was able to grab ahold of me and drag me out to the living room by my hair where we tussled more. All the while, I was fighting back. By this time, HE was injured and bleeding, and I would not let up. Finally, he picked me up and carried me to the back door where he threw me out of my own house and locked me outside on the terrace. I still had on pajamas, no shoes and no way to get back inside. He threw me over the terrace and locked the terrace door behind him. I landed in some bushes. Reluctantly, I knocked on my oldest daughter's bedroom window to ask her if she could let me in. I hated to even involve her. No parent would want to involve their children in something like this. It was, again, a low point for me emotionally. In the interim, he had thrown a few items of my clothing and my purse, which held very important information, into the woods behind our home. The depth of the woods made it impossible for me to go in and retrieve my personal belongings so, naturally, I was extremely upset by this time. She opened her bedroom window and I climbed inside, only to hear him on the phone calling 911. From the other side of the door, I could hear him conveniently telling the 911 operator that I had caused him bodily harm and that he'd like to have me arrested. "Is he serious?" I asked myself.

All three of my children were awake. I gathered the middle and youngest child and told them to barricade themselves in my oldest daughter's room and not to come out, no matter what they may hear. It was 9 am. They were supposed to be having breakfast and feeding their minds to prepare for school but, instead, they were witnessing a trauma the likes of which they had never seen or heard. I felt so awful and to this day, I cannot imagine how that day or witnessing any of this must have made them feel. A few moments later, County Police were at my door. The same officer who had responded in the previous weeks had also responded to this disturbance. We will just refer to him as "Officer Kyle." Officer Kyle arrived by himself, which was also out of the ordinary because whenever there was an officer response to a disturbance, there was always more than one unit. Officer Kyle separated us, pulled me outside, and left him inside of the apartment and asked me what happened. He said he already knew what happened because of our history of domestic disturbance calls but needed to obtain a statement from me anyway. I was completely upfront and honest with him about what had happened and told him that I was defending myself. He then went inside and took "his" statement. While Officer Kyle was speaking with him, I called Jaz because I just didn't have a good feeling. I knew that I was probably going to go to jail that day. I expected us both to be arrested, actually.

Officer Kyle came back outside after obtaining the other statement and, by the look he gave me, I knew that the day's events were about to worsen. He looked at me and said, "You know I don't want to take you but, I have to." I said, "Are you kidding me? I'm the victim. I was defending myself and as many times as I've called y'all out here to remove this man, you're going to arrest me? This is ridiculous!" "I know it. I don't want to take you as I said but, he displays visible signs of bodily harm and he is much more injured than you are. We have to take you," he said. "Wow," I replied. "Well, my three kids are inside. Can you just please wait until my friend gets here to take them? I don't want them to have to go to DFCS." "Sure thing," he replied. His response put my nerves at ease a little because it seemed that he was genuinely concerned about what happens to my children and didn't want to expose them to another traumatic event that day. Can you imagine how it would have affected you seeing your mother be taken away in hand-cuffs as a child? That's something that will never go away. I didn't want the burden of that memory being lodged into the brains of my babies for the rest of their lives. He didn't have to wait and he certainly could have just arrested me on the spot and let the system deal with my kids but he didn't, and for that I will forever feel gratitude for Officer Kyle.

About ten minutes later, Jaz arrived and man, she was pissed. Not at me but at the fact that all of this was even happening. Jaz is like me. She's a bulldog when she gets upset and anyone in her path will feel her wrath. It takes a lot to get her that way and, on that morning, she had finally reached the breaking point with my situation. You see, he was still talking shit. I mean, the entire time that I was standing outside waiting for her and talking with the officer, he was outside still talking down to me and taunting me about going to jail. He continued this behavior despite the officer's warnings for him to be quiet. Jaz got out of the car and immediately started going in! She always defends me and treats me as if I am her own flesh and blood, and I appreciate that more than she knows. The officer advised me to go inside and fetch my children so that he could get the arrest underway. I did as he asked. I brought them out and handed them over to Jaz along with the keys to my apartment and my debit card, and I instructed her to go inside and remove my WIFI box as well as my televisions. Did you think that I was going to allow this man to get me locked up, stay in my house, and relax comfortably after all this? Absolutely not. I then turned to the officer and pleaded, "Don't cuff me in front of my kids, please." He obliged and took me behind his patrol truck, which was parked adjacent to my apartment, and cuffed me there; out of the sight of my children. I wanted to cry so badly but I resisted as much as I could. I was going to jail for the first time in my life over some bullshit; over a man. How did I get here? What about my kids? What about my career? How will I ever explain this to my boss? What if they fire me? Who am I going to call? So many thoughts and worries went through my mind as I was sitting in the back of that patrol car and even then, I still would not allow myself to cry. Officer Kyle looked at me in the rearview mirror and said, "You're going to be okay. You don't have a record. I guarantee you will be processed out and back with your children before noon." I rode the rest of the ride in silence. Looking out of the window at the familiar scenery of the county I'd lived in. Staring at the people in the cars at the stop lights behind the tinted windows as they stared back in an attempt to see who was in the backseat. That overwhelming feeling and thought of "How did I get here? How did I end up on the other side of these tinted windows?" As we pulled into the parking lot of the jail, I felt knots in my stomach and lumps in my throat. Was I scared? Hell yeah! I had never been to jail a day in my life and up until this day, all I could do was imagine what was on the other side of those walls. He pulled to a stop and then turned back to look at me. He said, "I'm going to share something with you—when you get out of here, go to Live Safe Resources and request assistance with filing a TPO (Temporary Protective Order) immediately. When you get there, make sure you have all of your police reports and documentation of domestic incidents. This will be a way to keep him away from you until you can safely remove yourself and your kids from the apartment." "Okay, I will do that. Thank you," I replied. I said one thing to him but in my mind, I was thinking, "well, where was this information when I called y'all to my house these last 15 to 20 times?

Why wasn't this offered to me then? Why did you guys have to wait until the situation escalated to offer advice that was actually helpful to me as a victim of Domestic Violence?" I want to pause here because what I said is so crucial—officers need to be retrained on how to properly respond to Domestic Violence calls. There should be pamphlets available in their cruisers that list local resources, they should be separating the victim from the abusers to help him/her feel more comfortable speaking about what they've experienced, and they should also be able to quickly recite at least three local resources and options. A complete training overhaul is needed and if officers were properly trained, there may be more survivors saved on a daily basis. We count on them to protect us and uphold the law—they need to be doing just that.

As he walked me into the station, the lumps in my throat grew thicker and thicker. I could literally feel my knees shaking. The entire time the deputy was processing me into the system, everything was just a blur. After she was done she told me to go to the left, wait in a cell, and I would be able to enter the jail through a door on the other side. It was within those few minutes that I knew that I had to get myself together and toughen the fuck up, because I didn't know what resided on the other side of that door. Any fear that I had went away and I immediately went into survival mode. I heard a loud "BUZZZZZ" and the doors opened for me to enter. As I stepped inside, I immediately noticed that there were men and women housed in one sitting area in the jail with the men sitting on the left side and the women sitting on the right. "Take a seat!" the guard yelled from the desk to the right of me. I proceeded to walk to the sitting area and found a seat between two meth addicts. I was beginning to get angry because we were still in the beginning stages of a pandemic, and we didn't know much of anything about the virus. So naturally, I was concerned about germs and cleanliness.

"It's okay to be broken... Just know you can't stay there."

I felt disgusted. One of the women kept nodding off and slobbering all over the place. She began to lean over near me and I sternly told her she needed to lean herself back in the other direction (I won't include those exact words here). As I sat in that processing area for what seemed like an eternity, I was scoping out my surroundings and keeping my eyes on the clock that was on the wall directly in front of me. I kept asking myself how I would make a living if I lost my job; how can I ever get another job if I now have a criminal record? So many thoughts crossed my mind.

When I was finally given the opportunity to make my phone call, I called my mother. It took me a few tries before I was able to get through to her but when I finally did, naturally I was hysterical. I was rambling and told her that I was in jail and that I was defending myself because my ex had hit me. Her response to me was "I ain't trying to hear that mess, Katina. I ain't trying to hear it," and she hung up in my face. *I can't say that I was surprised, as our relationship had always been strained. That portion will be discussed later in the book. This may upset a lot of people but at the end of the day, it is my truth and no one can tell me what or how to feel. Although my mother and I have since repaired our relationship, the pain of her reaction to me that day will always stick with me.* I knew I couldn't call my siblings either. This would be just something else they would gossip about amongst each other. "Another failed relationship, here she goes again." My relationship with them was strained too if you will. *There have been times that I needed help be it emotionally or financially and it was looked at by them like I was just lying and asking for money when really, I barely made enough money to support one child, let alone two (at that time). I was really struggling in my early motherhood years with little to no help from my daughters' father. It was hard and I've had to make some pretty tough decisions just so we could survive. There was always a disconnect between*

38

my brothers and I anyway because there is a significant age gap between them and I. They are my seniors by more than ten years. I am also the only girl. Naturally, my feelings, emotions and thought process will always be different from theirs. When I came out and expressed certain things to them in the past about what I was going through, I was told "I'm crazy. I need to get over it," amongst many other insensitive things. These are people who don't fully understand trauma and how traumatic experiences during childhood can have long term effects. Any time I turned to them for help I ended up leaving feeling so emotionally invalidated. It sent me into a reclusive lifestyle. I just felt like I couldn't be vulnerable with anyone in that manner again which is why it made asking for help during the abusive relationship so difficult to do. It really sank in that day that I had nobody else but myself. So, I did the only other thing I could do and that was call Jaz and let her know to be on stand by as I should be released soon. I hung up the phone and made my way back to my seat. I just sat there, in my thoughts. Broken as fuck.

Some time had passed and at about 1:30pm, one of the officers said a judge had finally signed off on my bond order. I sat in jail for a total of 5 hours before they finally released me on my own recognizance. When my girl Jaz pulled up, she had some McDonald's waiting on a bihh. I was so angry and hungry all at the same time—I had gotten arrested before I even had a chance to eat breakfast! And all they served us were some dry ass ham sandwiches! I bit into the burger as if it were my last meal here on Earth. As I bit into the burger, my phone was turning on. It began to buzz with back to back text messages. I looked at my phone and it was him! "You've got to be fucking kidding me!" I yelled. *"Stink, I'm going crazy with you in there. My heart got locked up, yo. I want you tf outta there,"* the text message read. "This nigga is crazy! He the one who put me the fuck in there and now he's texting

"It's okay to be broken… Just know you can't stay there."

me?! Let me block this nigga." "Nah, don't do that," Jaz said. I looked over at her in the drivers seat like she was crazy and she stared back at me—then it was like a lightbulb turned on in my head. "Oh, I need to use his calls and texts as proof!" I said. "Bingo," Jaz replied. *Bet, I thought to myself and continued to eat my McDonald's.* We were headed to my home with a police escort to obtain some of my and the kids' belongings. I was going to stay at her house for a few days until I got all of this sorted out.

I AM STRONG

Think of a time when you had to be strong. What motivated you to stay strong? What are your greatest strengths? Write until you run out of space.

_____

_____

_____

_____

_____

_____

_____

_____

_____

_____

_____

_____

_____

_____

_____

_____

_____

_____

_____

Chapter 4: No Contact

Having supportive family and friends to be there for you like Jaz was for me is crucial during the no contact stage. During this time, you will likely be experiencing a whirlwind of emotions. Please know that feeling confused, vulnerable, and empathy for your abuser are all normal feelings. You are not alone in these thoughts. I can't identify with feeling empathy for my abuser, but I did feel very vulnerable and confused. That first night at Jaz's house, we watched *Basketball Wives*, drank wine, and went along as if everything were okay. But what she doesn't know is that night, I sat up lying on the floor in the guest bedroom of her townhouse, sobbing and screaming silently into the pillow. I was so hurt. Even more than that, I felt alone. Maybe she heard me, maybe she didn't. Either way, I cried myself to sleep that night but the next morning, I woke up and prayed. I prayed for the strength and courage to go through this next phase of my life—to remain strong in breaking free from him and doing everything in my power to make sure he stayed away from us. We got up and went straight to the local courthouse to apply for a TPO. When we got there, there was no one line, not even anyone waiting in the lobby. This made me feel a little more at ease because I was already somewhat embarrassed to be there in the first place. "Look girl, this is his 50th time calling me," I said to Jaz as we sat in the lobby of the county courthouse. "That nigga is crazy, yo. Hopefully the judge sees just how crazy he is." "I know, right," I replied.

"It's okay to be broken… Just know you can't stay there."

We waited for about 20 minutes for a representative to come to the desk. We had gotten there slightly early so we were okay with the wait. "HI there, did you need some help?" she asked. "Yes," I said. "My name is Katina Davis and I'm here to apply for a TPO. I have everything you need to know as it pertains to my situation right here in this folder, ma'am," I said as I passed her the folder through the small slot beneath the plexiglass. Things had become so weird with this COVID thing. Everyone was wearing masks now and talking behind temporary plexiglass or even long sheets of plastic wrap. It looked like something out of the Twilight Zone. On a regular day, the mask irritated me and I hated wearing it, but that day, I was happy to wear the mask. In some odd way, I felt safe behind it. "I see. I'll need you to take this clipboard and complete all documents in their entirety. Please try to be as detailed as possible." "Okay, will do. Thank you," I said. I sat back down in the seat to the right of Jaz and began to complete the required paperwork. Damn, man, I never thought I'd be in one of these places about to have these people all up in my business. One thing my Momma always taught me is *"the last thing you want is THEM FOLKS in your business."* I completed the paperwork and described every incident in detail as the representative had asked. *Before I go on, I want to share something with you about the forms you may complete as you apply for a TPO or anything else pertaining to family violence: READ THEM carefully. I had inadvertently consented to allowing the organization to refer my case to family and children's services. It was a yes or no question and had no bearing on the outcome of my TPO hearing. However, being in such a distraught state of mind and desperate to hurry the situation along, I checked yes in that box. Days later, there was a family and children's services rep walking into my home to verify my living conditions. It's crazy because had she arrived just thirty minutes earlier, she'd have found the house in disarray. The kids and I had just gotten home and fixed some of the damages in the apartment as a*

*result of our last incident. We hadn't been home up until that very minute that
the social worker had arrived.* So, from one mother to another, check no if
and when you see that question on a form. They can't deny your TPO based
on either answer.

"Okay, I think I've gotten everything completed," I said as I slid the
clipboard back under the plexiglass. "Okay. I'll just need you to sign these
last two pages, I'll sign and then I'll get it sent over to the judge for a hearing today." "Okay, cool." I sat back down in the chair next to Jaz, and we
both did the only thing we could really do at that point—wait. Lunchtime
had passed- the staff hidden behind the plexiglass had all gone to lunch and
come back and by this time, I was getting antsy. Finally, at about 1:30 in
the afternoon, I was called to appear before the judge in room 403. When I
entered the room, I noticed the sternness of the judge's face, his stringy gray
hair wreaking of old age and wisdom, and his demeanor of no nonsense.
"Katina Davis!" "Yes sir, present." "Why are you here today, Ms. Davis?" he
asked. I proceeded to explain the chain of events that led up to my applying
for the TPO on that day. As I spoke, I watched the way he took notes, then
looked back up at me over his glasses, which were on the brim of his nose. I
also had to include the fact that I had been arrested the day prior on battery
charges. I knew this wouldn't help my case and as I suspected, it didn't. The
judge looked at me and said, "Well, it sounds to me like you're looking for a
quick eviction. Your TPO is denied." I nearly lost my footing standing at that
podium. I couldn't believe what I had just heard. The representative that took
my application looked back at me from the front of the courtroom with such
sorrow and pity in her eyes and mouthed the words "I'm sorry." I didn't even
give the judge the opportunity to finish his statement. I quickly snatched my
purse from the seat where Jaz sat and stormed out of the courtroom, my eyes

"It's okay to be broken... Just know you can't stay there."

filled with tears. Jaz stepped out of the courtroom right behind me and began to say something that to this day, I don't remember. Everything that happened after the judge made that ruling was quite a blur. We hurried through the halls, quickly turning each corner until we'd made it to the ground floor and out the front door of the courthouse. The cry I let out once I was out of that building, I'll never forget. Defeated. Once again. Psalms 123 says, "I look to the hills from whence cometh my help. My help cometh from the Lord." That verse rang in my spirit the entire way home. By home I meant Jaz's. At the moment, I didn't have a home. The man who was the cause of all of this turmoil had taken over my home and there was absolutely nothing I could do about it. *I guess this portion of what I was going through with him could be considered Economic Abuse. Economic Abuse is a form of abuse when one intimate partner has control over the other partner's access to economic resources. Of course, I was not aware of all the aspects of what I was experiencing while I was in the situation but knowing what I know now; it's a miracle I made it away from that man in one piece and of sound mind. He was absolutely insane.*

By 8pm that night, my phone had over 100 text messages and 500 missed calls. *Statistics state that a survivor is most in danger within the first three months of exiting the relationship. Especially when the survivor goes no contact with the abuser despite their efforts to get them back. This makes the abuser feel that they've lost control over you and the situation/relationship. Their anger and rage will begin to build and they will become enraged over the fact that you are ignoring them. It's important not to give in to their efforts after you've made the decision to exit the relationship. Stick to your guns and choose yourself and your happiness. You've got this. I'm not telling you anything that I didn't have to do myself. It won't be easy. But it can certainly be done.* A few days had passed and I needed to go back home and obtain some clothing to hold us over a little while longer while we were at Jaz's. I was praying he was either gone or had killed himself. It had been a full 24 hours and I hadn't received any calls or texts from him. As we came nearer to my apartment at the top of the hill, I was able to see that he was standing on the front steps of the building singing and listening to music. "Oh God," I said to myself. "Here we go." I hopped out of the jeep with all intent of walking straight past him as if he weren't even there, but he wouldn't be him if he didnt talk shit in the process. "Oh, you broke bitch. I bleached your clothes. You're going to be real sorry." I continued to ignore him and walked into my home where I noticed that he had cut the cord on my big screen television, poured bleach in the back of it, and bleached several items of my clothing including a Rest In Peace shirt that reflected my deceased niece—she had died a year prior and that shirt was one of its kind. I could never get that back. Him destroying that t-shirt that day is what hurt me the most; and he knew it. I continued to walk through to the back of the apartment to the room that he and I shared. I noticed something that I didn't expect to see. His side of the closet was completely empty. It seems he had left the apartment willingly, but why was he still lingering around my house? My first initial thought was that he had somehow found a homeless shelter and I had pulled up just at the end of him gathering his things. Whatever the case was, he was out of my house. I contacted the police to report harassment but by the time they had arrived, he had gone.

Jaz and I figured he was long gone, so she helped us settle back into our home, change the locks, and we essentially just left her place and went back home. The kids and I were happy to be back in our own beds, with our own precious things and possessions. About two days went by and I had been continuing to receive random text messages from him asking to reconcile, but I continued to ignore his advances. I had intended on filing for a TPO

"It's okay to be broken… Just know you can't stay there."

again and this time, I would win because I knew that the evidence would be overwhelming. He just couldn't help himself and wouldn't leave me alone. *Please be sure to document all incidents, even if it is just a shove. You need to be able to have a paper trail when it comes time to protect yourself in a court of law. I don't want what happened to me to happen to anyone else. I cried out for help so many times, and my cries were repeatedly ignored.*

I was coming back from the grocery store, two days after my kids and I had moved back into the apartment, and I nearly ran into another car because I saw him coming out of my building with my neighbor and he had gotten into the passenger seat of his car. "Oh my God!" I yelled. "All this fucking time! He's been in there all this time?!" This was the last place on Earth I'd ever thought that he would be! My neighbor turned out to be from the same area he and I are from and once he found that out, he and the guy were always hanging together. The guy was at least ten years younger than him—he was always befriending younger guys, which was honestly a red flag for me early on in the relationship. I always wondered why someone who was almost 40 years old couldn't attract and cling to positive male figures his own age. My guess is because they could be easily manipulated. *Always trust your gut and pay attention to the signs.*

When I saw him come out of that building, I got stuck for a second. I was unsure what to do. He looked toward my car with this condescending grin. He was just so evil. "What the hell?!" I said for what had to be the 50th time. I called my kids to come out and get the groceries from the trunk. I didn't say anything to them about seeing him because I didn't want to alarm them. I sent them inside and then I sat in the car and made a call to Jaz. "Hello?" she answered. "Bitch! Guess where the fuck he been at this entire time! " "Where?" she asked. "He's been at the neighbor's house; the one that's from where we're from." Wowwww," she said. "I know, right. I don't know what to do now," I replied. I didn't stay in the car and talk to her for long because I wanted to get back inside in case he came back. I just wanted to be able to tell her enough so that she knows exactly who did it and a timeline if something happened to me. It was that serious and I had an eerie feeling in the pit of my stomach.

A few hours later, I got a knock on the door. I looked out of the peephole, it was him. He was knocking on the door saying he smelled my cooking and begged for a plate because he hadn't eaten in days. I told him to get away from my door and threatened to call the police. I thought he was going to get erratic and start screaming in the hallway but he didn't. He continued to talk through the door in the softest tone—it was strange and unlike him to speak in such a calm manner. I was getting scared because I didn't know what his state of mind was. I just let him talk to himself through the door and continued not to respond. All through the night, he knocked on my back window begging me to let him in on top of calling my phone repeatedly. I lived on the ground floor and I was fearful that he would eventually reach his breaking point and break the window. Instead, he stood outside of the window and called my phone over 100 times. Over 100 times within a 4-hour time frame. It was the wee hours of the night when all the neighbors were sleeping. I called the police and reported the harassment, but he had disappeared once again by the time they arrived. I took the police report and went to bed because I was deliriously tired at that point. I hadn't properly slept in nearly a week and my body just gave out that morning.

I came outside the next morning to run an errand, and my daughter noticed that the back tire on the right side of my car was flat. I said, "Ain't no way! I just replaced that tire!" I didn't think anything of it at the time. I'm

"It's okay to be broken... Just know you can't stay there."

famous for buying used tires, so I figured I had hit a speed bump at some point. I contacted my insurance company, and they sent roadside to replace the tire with my spare. I went on about my day and didn't give it another thought. I also hadn't received any calls from him, so I thought I was in the clear. Once again, I was wrong. He saw my car sitting outside of a local nail salon and walked into the nail salon to demand that I talk to him. I was looking down signing my receipt to pay, and when I looked up he was literally standing right up on me, next to the pedicure bowl. I looked at my nail tech and gave her a look that suggested I was uncomfortable. She asked him to leave.

Is anyone else seeing a pattern here? I was being stalked by an abusive, mentally unstable person who had previously attempted to take his own life. Yet, they denied my request for a TPO. That man could have killed me so many times but by the grace of God, he could never get to me when I was by myself. The following morning after Geico came and put the donut on my car, I noticed that the tire on the other side of my car was now flat. "Hold up, this ain't no coincidence," I said. "Somebody is doing this." I then contacted Geico again and this time, reported vandalism. A tow truck came pretty quickly; about 15 minutes after I discovered the second flat tire. I explained to him what had happened and he said, "Okay. Watch this. I'm going to help you out." He took an air hose from beneath his tow truck and began to pump air into my tire. As he began to pump the air, he and I both noticed that the air was coming out as fast as he was putting it in. It was then that the tow truck driver and I both noticed that the tire was slashed. He said, "Ma'am, someone did this on purpose." At that point, I contacted the police to make an official police report. I had also started crying. I just didn't understand why he was doing this. Why couldn't he just leave me alone?! He had cost me so much already, and I don't mean just financially. He and his demons were like a leech; draining me for everything I had spiritually and emotionally. All this because I finally have the courage to say that I want out and am standing on that decision. I was tired. I was so tired.

After the officer took the report, I accompanied the tow truck driver to a local tire shop to repair my tire. The tow truck driver had an idea what I was going through and decided to stick around the tire shop to make sure the guys there did a thorough job and didn't give me any trouble. They changed the tire in about twenty minutes and I headed back to my apartment. As I entered the complex and drove to the top hill, what I saw had me lost for words. This man was in front of my house talking to the police. I knew I hadn't called the police so what could they possibly be doing there? I was even more speechless when I actually heard what it was that he was saying to them. He told them that I had put him out and forced him from the home where he was a resident. *Lie #1- He left willingly. If you recall, I stated earlier in the chapter that when I got home his side of the closet was empty, remember?* This was just another piece to his puzzle of narcissistic abuse and games. Everything was just happening so fast. I was struggling to keep up with the lies he was telling and even more astonished by how the police were just feeding into his lies. I had done my best to maintain no contact with this man, but he was literally stalking me; harassing me; trying to force his way back into my life using his manipulative tactics and the police were just letting it happen. It was unbelievable and this is why so many Domestic Violence situations become fatal. Some of them can be avoided.

Over 45 minutes had passed and by that time, the leasing office and nearly everyone else that lived in my court was outside on the pavement watching the show. Their entertainment was my living hell. The police ended up siding with him and demanded that I allow him back into the premises. My children and I left right then with only the clothes on our backs and checked into the hotel that we'd stayed in on previous occasions. I had made it into the hotel parking lot when all of a sudden my car began to sputter then soon shut off. My oldest daughter was able to step out of the car before I was. "Ma, there's something leaking from your tank." "What do you mean?" I asked. I walked around to the other side of the car and opened the gas cap. The gas tank was filled with sugar. What kind of man would do something like this? I'm the sole provider for these kids! All of this because I don't want to be with you?! I was livid. All I could remember was pacing back and forth in the hotel parking lot, crying, unable to withhold my emotions for the sake of my children. I was just overwhelmed. It was all too much. He was getting more dangerous and I knew eventually he would do me harm. I checked my kids into the hotel and had a friend sit with them, and I set off to go apply for another TPO. Only this time I wasn't timid and afraid. I was pissed.

Once again, the halls and lobby of the county TPO office were empty. You could hear the stomp of my shoe as I rapidly approached the little window with the plexiglass. "Yo, you remember me? I was here last week. Y'all denied my TPO but look what has happened to me since then," I yelled. *Slap!* I had slapped a purple folder filled with printouts of threats through text messages, call logs, emails, a statement from the nail tech stating he followed me to the nail salon, amongst many other things. The same representative that did my intake previously was there again on that day. She said, "Yes, I remember you. You have to fill out another application. You can go into detail, but I have all your documentation. This folder should be enough." I completed the paperwork and was mindful to check "No" when I got to the family and children's services question. They won't get me a second time. I scanned over the paperwork to ensure that I had included everything, and it was all there. She processed my request for a TPO and I went before a judge for the second time to have my plea heard. The TPO was granted that time—by a woman who looked just like me. The TPO was served to him an hour later, and he violated it two hours later. He was finally apprehended and charged accordingly for his crimes.

I am WORTHY

What are some things that you have wanted to experience/gain in your life? What steps have you taken to get there? If you have not yet taken any steps to become closer to your goal, what is your action plan to make it happen? Write until you run out of space.

_____

_____

_____

_____

_____

_____

_____

_____

_____

_____

_____

_____

_____

_____

_____

_____

_____

Chapter 5: Healing

The system failed me. So many times. I could have been dead or worse on a number of occasions, and I'm sure that is a reality for many of you. Most abusers repeatedly go to extremes to prevent the victim from leaving. As I previously stated, leaving an abusive relationship is the most dangerous time for a victim of domestic violence. There was one study found in interviews with men who have killed their wives showing that threats of separation or, their wives actually leaving were more likely to be the precipitating events that led to the murder. If you are in an abusive relationship, it is my hope that me sharing my truth will help put a mirror up in front of you. I pray that it touched you in some way and that you are inspired to give yourself a chance to live—a chance to flourish—a chance to become. You haven't even found the best of you yet and there is so much more about yourself that you need to learn about and let the world see. The beautiful parts of me were brought out AFTER surviving my experience. I can say that surviving domestic violence inspired me to become a better version of myself.

After the dust had settled, I had begun to attend therapy. God, that was such an ugly process. Some days I would literally want to hug my therapist and others, I wanted to fight her! Whew, she would read me like an old tarot mother in the bayou! I am grateful that I chose to attend therapy. Shortly after I started seeing her, I was formally diagnosed with PTSD (Post Traumatic Stress Disorder). *PTSD is "a disorder in which a person has difficulty recovering after experiencing or witnessing a terrifying event."* Domestic Violen-

"It's okay to be broken… Just know you can't stay there."

ce of any kind does qualify as a terrifying event. As we all know, Domestic Violence can come in many forms—Emotional, Physical or Economic.. The effects of PTSD can sometimes be long lasting, which is why it is only treatable by a medical professional. I know there's a major negative stigma attached to therapy in the black community. But I'm here to tell you that that stigma couldn't be more wrong. Therapy is not a bad word. Therapy is a very important step in the healing process after leaving an abusive relationship. Know that you can't and don't have to get through this alone.

While going through therapy, I began to address certain traumas that I endured throughout my life but at some point had forgotten about. Therapy has a funny way of doing that to you. You seek out a therapist for assistance with one problem but find yourself addressing issues that you didn't even realize you had. Sometimes, the experiences and problems we encounter throughout our adult lives are a direct result of childhood trauma and experiences during childhood and adolescence. Then, at some point, we sit down and ask ourselves the really hard questions— *"Why did I do this? Why did I allow him/her around? Why can't I let people get close to me? What's wrong with me? Why don't I trust anyone? Why do I keep reliving the same experiences?"* Therapy made me ask some of these questions and many others—the answer was deeply rooted in my childhood and adolescence. At the age of four years old, I was molested by the teenage son of a family friend. My mother's friend ran a daycare out of her home which wasn't uncommon in the early 90's. Her sons and I were often in the back in the bedroom from what I can recollect. Whose bedroom it was exactly, i cannot recall. While I do not want to revisit that day detail by detail, I am willing to say that I was fondled directly on my vagina with his penis. There was no penetration that I can remember. This activity was unusual enough to me that I felt compelled to tell my mother.

As a tender four-year-old girl, I knew something wasn't right about that and that it wasn't supposed to be happening. My mother removed me from the daycare and never took me back there again. When I finally revealed this information to my father as an adult, he disclosed to me that he never knew. My mother never told him. He also said that I was the only girl attending the daycare at that time and that he communicated with my mother that he was uncomfortable with my being there surrounded by all boys. "I'm so sorry baby. I didn't know. I didn't know," he said. Hearing his voice crack over the phone as if he was holding back tears, that hurt me more than words could ever express.

As I went through life, I did continue to vividly remember what had happened to me. Yet somehow well into my adult years I had forgotten all about it until around New Year's of 2019. I began to dream about that day from my childhood and had decided to call my mother to ask her about it. She confirmed that those dreams were in fact my reality as a child. My therapist suspects that this memory re-presented itself due to the escalation in trauma during my abusive relationship. When the physical violence escalated is when I began to dream about being molested. Man, when I talked to my therapist about this particular occurrence, I just cried. There was nothing else I could do but cry. I had no idea that the four-year-old girl inside of me was still hurting. I didn't realize what an impact that day would turn out to have on me. It was a tough thing to face and an even tougher thing to heal from. I was forced to forgive someone I barely remember, someone I don't even remember knowing. That was the most agonizing part of all. Not being able to confront them or receive an apology. But I learned in therapy that healing isn't for the person who hurt you, the healing is for you. There's a saying that

"It's okay to be broken… Just know you can't stay there."

goes "Although your wounds aren't your fault, healing is absolutely your responsibility," and that couldn't be more true.

Make no mistakes—the healing process is long, and it's ugly. Don't feel any pressure to heal at anyone else's pace but your own. Your healing may not look like everyone else's and that's completely okay. It took me eighteen years to heal from the hurt and pain of my mother's absence during my teen years. She and my dad divorced at a very important time in a young woman's life—my freshman year of high school. I was a Daddy's girl to the core. So, when they divorced it was extremely hard on me. I started acting out, having sex, and skipping school. A once 3.0 GPA student had turned into a 1.15 GPA student and I was heading nowhere fast. My mom at the time had moved on relatively quickly and had a new man in her life. That man is now her husband. She ended up putting me out of the house and sending me away to go and live with one of my older brothers when I was 15 years old. She said it was either that or she was going to "put me in the system." I wasn't mature enough to comprehend what was happening between her, my father, and her moving on so quickly with this new man but I knew enough to know that she should have been clinging to me during that time, not sending me away. I had just lost my father in a sense. I needed support and guidance from her.

In many ways I feel that was the pivotal point in my life—when it took a wrong turn. By not having my mother around, I was out looking for the love in men that I really wanted to receive from her. I spent years—boyfriend after boyfriend—searching for something that no one else could really give me. I hated myself. I hated my past. I hated my life. I really did and I was trying to numb that pain by looking for someone to love me. Not realizing that I must first learn to love myself. How you feel about yourself is a direct reflection of how others will treat you. I didn't know my worth.

I didn't have anyone around to teach me those things as a young woman coming of age—I lacked the maternal guidance that I felt I needed in order to successfully navigate a monogamous relationship with a man. I also didn't have an example of a healthy relationship throughout my childhood either. I witnessed years of infidelity on my Dad's part and escalated arguments in between. My mom stuck by my father for years throughout his unfaithfulness when she probably should have chosen herself. Not probably—she definitely should have chosen herself. No woman has to accept that treatment. No one period should accept anything less than what they deserve. My Mom is a strong woman and the things she endured throughout her life would have probably brought me to my knees. I respect the woman she is and the woman she continues to become. Without her, there would be no me and I am proud to be her daughter.

Healing my relationship with my mom was a game changer—therapy as well as finally talking to my mom from a calm and peaceful space helped me to realize that she had her own story to tell and that I needed to show her a little grace. I learned some things about my Mother—about my lineage. I learned that Domestic Violence preceded me. My Mother is a survivor, my grandmother was a survivor as well as many other matriarchs in my family. My Mom had a very rough childhood—one that lacked the proper love, care, and affection that should be shown to a child. She was taught that strength and vulnerability can't dwell in the same place and unknowingly implemented that theory into her parenting. I was raised rough, man—like a boy. Again, I am the youngest of all boys so she did the best she could and raised me the very way she raised them. I had a chance to process the fact that she couldn't give me something that she didn't receive as a child herself which also may ring true for some of you. I know now that her parenting style was only a reflection of the way she was raised. I forgave her. I forgive her. Therapy helped me do that. After I was able to heal my relationship with my Mother, it seemed as if my whole outlook on life changed. I learned to create and maintain healthy boundaries—something I struggled with for years. I learned that no one, no matter their title, is allowed to make me feel inferior or tell me that my feelings are not valid. I learned that I have a voice. I learned that I'm a good person. I learned how to love myself enough so that I'm not looking for love from anyone else. I learned to get to know ME. Things I used to accept from others, I no longer accept. I am no longer worried about what people think of me—if they like me or don't like me. None of that matters anymore. I LIKE ME.

I emerged from this process an unapologetic butterfly and I am thankful to have gone through the fire. My experience was building me, molding me for something greater in life, guiding me into my purpose—to teach, educate, lead and inspire other young women and girls all around the world. To encourage you all to use your voices, educate you on the warning signs, help you find your self-worth and to share with you the tools that I've learned on how to properly love yourself. My purpose was always greater than me—and had it not been for going through the abuse, I may have never found it. I am now the founder of a non-profit organization whose sole purpose is to empower victims and survivors of Domestic Violence; providing preventative education, community resources and long-term support. Every day I am inspired and led to be inspired because I continue to encounter such phenomenal women along this journey. So if you learned nothing else from this book, please know this: YOU ARE STRONG. YOU ARE BEAUTIFUL. YOU ARE AMAZING. YOU ARE WORTHY. Don't you ever forget it and if you have, that's okay. I lost sight of those things too for a while but guess what, I had a friend there to pull the blindfold off and now here I am, being that friend to you. It's amazing to me that what was supposed to break me made me ten times stronger. Always remember: It's okay to be broken; just know you can't stay there."

If you or someone you know is experiencing Domestic Violence, please contact the National Domestic Violence hotline at 1-800-799-SAFE.